Praise for *Nuggets for Teens*

"Murween Rose has concisely and beautifully given teen-agers these nuggets of practical and empowering life skills. If only I had this when I was a teenager! These helpful tips are easy to read and glance at for those busy times as a teenager, when things can feel overwhelming. The insight Murween gives, will last a lifetime. I highly recommend it to anyone who is a teenager or has teenagers since the information presented will be useful on both sides."

—Mourette Valcin, BA Reconciliation Studies

"Murween Rose, I applaud you for making the decision to publish a book for teenagers and pre-teenagers. It is indeed relevant, necessary, and absolutely timely. This book has analyzed and identified all the practical issues associated with teenagers and pre-teenagers, as many of them grapple with peer pressure and their parents' expectations. You have given much assistance in areas of making personal decisions, setting goals for achievements, and personal development."

—I. Campbell, Teacher

"After reading only a few chapters, it is clear that this book is written well. There are many interesting, intriguing, and helpful pointers for teens. I particularly like that the "nuggets" are in a list format. This makes the content very attractive to the intended audience. Overall, I believe this book will be helpful to both teenagers and their parents. Bravo, another well written book by this author!

—GRT, Business Administration

"This book provides some valuable tips which, if adapted by young ones, can serve to empower those who read these nuggets. I commend Murween for taking the time out to write so creatively. Drawing from one's experience and knowledge can also be extremely effective. I definitely recommend your book to readers."

—J. Gordon, Nurse

Nuggets for Teens

A Friendly Guide to Navigating Your Teen Years

Murween Perry-Rose

Aquarrhire Press

Illinois

Aquarrhire Press
Illinois

Publisher's Note: This book is prepared solely for informational and educational purposes, and not for therapy. Please seek professional help for any issues you are facing that are overwhelming.

Book Layout © 2017 BookDesignTemplates.com
Editing and Layout by Jeanne Felfe—Jeannefelfe.com

Nuggets for Teens/ Murween Perry-Rose. -- 1st ed.
ISBN 978-17366854-0-2

To my daughters
for their unwavering support and
encouragements.

You are a star!
There is a gift in everyone
and there is one in you.

Contents

Foreword

OVER THE YEARS, NUMEROUS books have been written expressing how to be a good person, a good teen, and basically the best human being one can possibly be. Here is a book that is simply inspirational and written specifically for the emergent teen. It is filled with practical suggestions that can assist teenagers as they weather the storms of adolescence and transition safely to the next phase of their lives, as well-adjusted adults. This book is easy to read and filled with workable solutions for almost every problem common to the average teenager. It is certainly a must have for teens—one they can truly call their own. The challenges teenagers face are real and as a result they need guidance. These nuggets are geared toward the holistic development of teens.

This book provides information I am positive can change the lives of adolescents in a most positive and dynamic way with practice. Murween Rose is one who writes from her heart. It is her deepest desire to see young people achieve and become well-rounded citizens, who will make something of their lives and make a positive impact on the growth and development of this society.

Beyond the shadow of a doubt, Murween is blazing the trail as she speaks profoundly to the hearts of many through her prolific writing. I believe the Guidance and Counseling fraternity is indeed blessed to have such a warm-hearted and inspirational human being heralding their cause as she makes it known that wellness can be achieved in every area of our lives: Children need to be well; parents need to be well; and of course teenagers need to be well.

Patrice Small, Teacher

Preface

THESE NUGGETS WILL BE a rich addition to the many resources already available to help teenagers grow and develop as great men and women. They also provide workable suggestions geared toward revealing a teenager's true self. The teenage years can be frightening, but with the proper guidance teens can be successful. As a counselor, I am faced with myriad questions from parents and teenagers. In a workshop with some parents, the question was asked, *"Which age and stage do you dread most with your child?"* About 85% of the parents shouted, *"The teenage stage."* When asked why, they replied:

- The teen years can be very scary
- It can be exciting
- I can't manage the tantrums
- Teens sometimes don't listen
- They love to have their own way
- They are sometimes disobedient, demanding, and rebellious

Do any of these actions sound familiar?

There are parents who may relate to one or most of these. While some parents thought of the difficulties, there were those who hastened to comment that the adolescent stage can be cool if parents demonstrate a level of understanding and communicate with them fairly. If parents inculcate the right values in their teens, they will be remembered through their different stages of development. Many parents are also concerned that their teen may engage in risky behaviors in order to get the approval of their peers. While this may be true, there are those teens who are mannerly, kind, respectful, obedient, disciplined, and very conscious of what they are doing and what they would like to achieve in life. I believe that amidst the turmoil and challenges teenagers face, they can still become the very best in life. To all teenagers, I hope that when you are not certain of what to do, or how to behave, you will talk with your parents, or someone you trust. You can also reach out to your social workers and school counselors.

The world is changing and so are teenagers. Someone must help in guiding the process to assist teens as they navigate their way through the teenage years. It is unfortunate that some teenagers have to struggle to deal with life issues on their own due to lack of guidance. As a result, some teens seem to grow up quickly with the pain of discovering who they are. These nuggets are geared toward providing tips and information for helping teens as they grow and develop into great citizens.

Murween Perry-Rose

Nugget 1

∗

School Life Challenges

TEENAGERS AND PRE-TEENS GOING off to middle and high school experience fulfilling moments, but they also experience some of the most challenging times in their lives. During this phase, without appropriate guidance and a stable home with caring parents or guardians, teenagers can get lost in the mix of dealing with peer pressures, the various changes going on developmentally and at school. There are many tips a teen can apply to deal with various issues.

Here are some tips that can help:

- ❖ Be yourself
- ❖ Do not allow anyone to define who you are
- ❖ Try being strong and courageous instead of being scared
- ❖ Do not try to please all your friends
- ❖ Never try to be someone else
- ❖ Develop friendships with those who enjoy your company
- ❖ Create a good work ethic so you can maintain good grades
- ❖ Be on time for your classes
- ❖ Study hard; it will be rewarding
- ❖ Turn in your assignments on time
- ❖ Follow your teachers' guidance in class for academic success
- ❖ Try and display the appropriate behaviors while in school
- ❖ Try to be polite and respectful to members of staff. Respect does not cause you to lose your rights; it enhances them

❖ Be involved in at least one school-based activity such as clubs, sports, or after-school programs, if at all possible

❖ Do not be dependent on peers for your own happiness. Enjoy your life and learn as much as you can!

Conclusion:

Moving on to middle or high school is a new experience, one that is filled with new challenges and goals. It is important for you to keep in mind why you are at school. Study wisely. Have fun! Be yourself and work to the best of your ability. If for any reason you are not managing well, always talk with a trusted adult including your social worker or school counselors.

You are a star!

You are destined for great things in life.
Never lose sight of your goals!

Reflection, Notes or Journal:

_____
_____
_____
_____
_____
_____
_____
_____
_____
_____
_____
_____
_____
_____

Nugget 2

✿

Demonstrating Positive Behaviors in School

POSITIVE BEHAVIORS IN SCHOOL are those qualities that depict wholesomeness. They allow you to feel good about yourself and others, while others are left feeling good about you. I am aware that sometime school and community culture can be challenging, but you can be a shining star even if others don't believe you are. It is all about being you and standing up for yourself. Positive behaviors enable you to live a worthwhile life in and out of school and can assist you in being a role model to your peers, and within your community.

Tips that can help:

- ❖ Be on time for class
- ❖ Demonstrate good social skills
- ❖ Be respectful to your teachers and peers
- ❖ Develop good working habits
- ❖ Be courteous
- ❖ Be honest
- ❖ Never be labeled a bully
- ❖ Be kind in your actions and words
- ❖ Do your assignments and follow through with the due dates
- ❖ Say no to drugs and gangs or gang-related activities
- ❖ Engage in extra-curricular activities
- ❖ Join an outreach organization in your community
- ❖ Be the best person you can be

Conclusion:

As teenagers, the major focus in school should be to learn your lessons well, have fun, have a mind of your own, and be your best self. Be proud of your achievements and allow your parents to be proud of you. If you fail in any way, do not stay down: get up and try again. You can surely make it, if you keep on trying. Be patient with yourself and go get good grades. Do not stress!

Having the right attitude works
well with success.

Reflection, Notes or Journal:

_____

_____

_____

_____

_____

_____

_____

_____

_____

_____

_____

_____

_____

_____

_____

Nugget 3

Owning My
Self-Esteem

SELF-ESTEEM IS A FEELING of satisfaction about who you are. The term is further used to describe a teen's overall sense of self-worth or self-value.

Owning your self-esteem can be a positive influence on your life. The development of a positive self-esteem is especially important for teenagers in making a successful transition from one stage to another.

Here are some suggestions to assist in keeping your self-esteem intact:

- ❖ Use "I Statements" with confidence and be proud of who you are
- ❖ Love yourself and the person you are and are becoming
- ❖ If you experience unfortunate events in life, do not focus on them forever. Instead, set goals and keep on working to achieve them.
- ❖ Focus on your strengths (the things you are good at)
- ❖ If you identify weaknesses, try learning from them and move on
- ❖ Be appreciative of life and know what you want for your life
- ❖ Enjoy positive peer relationships and stay away from the negative ones
- ❖ Do not speak down to yourself
- ❖ Do not accept the negatives others throw at you
- ❖ Say NO to wrong thoughts

- ❖ Develop a good self-care attitude for yourself
- ❖ Keep a simple journal of the things you enjoy about your life each day

Conclusion:

The ability to maintain a positive self-esteem can be a roller-coaster ride for teenagers, but always remember the thought of believing in yourself and your efforts as you go through each day. No matter what your daily challenges may look like, or what others may say in a negative way, always think well of yourself. Self-esteem is something you should always take with you and utilize in good or in difficult times.

Never accept NO when moving forward
with your goals simply because someone tells
you that you can't.

Reflection, Notes or Journal:

_____
_____
_____
_____
_____
_____
_____
_____
_____
_____
_____
_____
_____
_____
_____

Nugget 4

✤

Building My
Self-Confidence

SELF-CONFIDENCE IS BELIEVING in your-self and in your abilities to shine. Believing in your abilities can give you a sense of self-worth and boldness. Self-confidence can also be developed by having a belief system that helps you to perform a task in a successful way. Having confidence can help you to face and overcome your fears and handle any situation you will experience. For teens who are shy and of an introverted personality, don't get too worried as self-confidence can develop overtime.

Here are some tips that can help:

- ❖ Practice positive self-talk
- ❖ Do not compare yourself to others
- ❖ Think positively
- ❖ Be brave even when it is hard to do so
- ❖ Know your strengths and limitations
- ❖ Stay away from inferiority complex (which is more like feeling inadequate).
- ❖ Believe in yourself
- ❖ Be comfortable in your own skin
- ❖ Love yourself
- ❖ Respect yourself
- ❖ Maintain eye contact when speaking to someone
- ❖ Be self-assured and less insecure
- ❖ Believe in your ability

Conclusion:

Self-confidence will help you think confidently about yourself and encourage a more positive attitude to do tasks that you are asked to do. This skill does not happen all at once, but is developed through a step-by-step process as you grow.

Own your Self-confidence without trying
to convince anyone that you have it!

Reflection, Notes or Journal:

_____

_____

_____

_____

_____

_____

_____

_____

_____

_____

_____

_____

_____

_____

_____

_____

Nugget 5

❧

Owning My Values

THERE ARE VARIOUS TYPES of value systems established in a society as standards to guide behaviors. As teens, your foundation values are generated mostly from your home. Others can be formed or learned through the community and school environment. Your personal value system gives you structure and a purpose by helping you to determine what is meaningful and important to life. It can also assist you in expressing who you are and what you stand for. It can be a beautiful feeling to own your values and be proud of them as a teenager. Never be afraid to add to the values that your parents and guardians have inculcated in you. Whatever those are, with careful evaluation of right and wrong, define them and embrace them!

Other values that can enhance personal development:

- ❖ Respect yourself and others
- ❖ Help others when you can
- ❖ Be honest
- ❖ Be fair in your decisions
- ❖ Show empathy to others
- ❖ Value justice and equality
- ❖ Learn how to forgive when others hurt you
- ❖ Forgive yourself when you make a mistake
- ❖ Be courageous
- ❖ Be dutiful
- ❖ Show compassion to others
- ❖ Appreciate yourself and others
- ❖ Be at peace with yourself and your friends
- ❖ Be dependable the best way you can

❖ Be caring
❖ Be self-aware
❖ Have a sense of humor
❖ Be a good citizen
❖ Be loyal
❖ Develop good friendships

Conclusion:

Regardless of your own personal list of values, if you believe in them, embrace them! The above list is one you can examine, evaluate, and use if needed for personal development.

A good value system can be incredibly important to take you through the world as you grow and develop.

Reflection, Notes or Journal:

_____

_____

_____

_____

_____

_____

_____

_____

_____

_____

_____

_____

_____

_____

Nugget 6

❧

Thinking Positively About Yourself

HAVING A POSITIVE OUTLOOK on life often comes from intrinsic motivation. A teen's ability to think positively and behave in a positive manner in some cases hinges on his or her environment and parenting styles. Resilient teens are often able to beat the odds and aspire to believe in themselves regardless of life challenges.

Some tips that can help you in staying positive:

- ❖ Always love yourself
- ❖ Do not try to be another person

- ❖ Tell yourself, you will be the best you
- ❖ Have a positive outlook on your life
- ❖ Try not to let negative thoughts overwhelm you
- ❖ Enjoy laughter with your friends and family
- ❖ Be proud of your achievements
- ❖ Be your best friend if no one else will
- ❖ Have an "I can do it attitude" about the goals you set for your life
- ❖ Affirm yourself along the journey
- ❖ Believe that you are destined for greatness
- ❖ Get involved in sports and other clubs
- ❖ Be optimistic about life even with its challenges
- ❖ Talk with individuals who are positive
- ❖ See challenges as a motivational factor for being successful in everything you do
- ❖ Know what your values are and celebrate them

Conclusion:

One way to be positive is to believe in yourself and in your potential and fostering positive relationships. It is also important that you stay optimistic about life and know that life will not always be smooth. Whenever you are faced with challenges, reflect on the coping skills you have and use them to assist you in that situation. Always remember that your actions begin with a thought. Let that thought be a positive one and believe it.

Life is always moving on, be aware of
where it is taking you!

Reflection, Notes or Journal:

_____

_____

_____

_____

_____

_____

_____

_____

_____

_____

_____

_____

_____

_____

_____

_____

_____

Nugget 7

Setting Goals for Success

GOAL SETTING CAN BE defined as a process of identifying something you want to accomplish and plan with a time-frame in mind to achieve it. Practicing the art of setting goals at this stage is a good training experience that will help you in college and for all other aspects of your life.

❖ Choose one goal at a time and work the best you can to achieve it. If you would like to get an "A" in Social Studies or any other subject, write down what you need to do to get that grade and work toward achieving it.

❖ If you would like to be a professional or a successful basketball player now or later, write it down and create the steps you need to take to be successful.

Here is an example of an acronym called CLEVER goals:

Clever Goals can be a helpful guide to work toward the goals you set for your life, whether life, whether academic or personal.

✓ **C**—Create a plan around a specific goal

✓ **L**—learn ways to develop short or long term goals; for example, write down what you would like to achieve within a specific time period or within a school term.

✓ **E**—Evaluate what is needed to accomplish that goal, for example, what resources and support will be needed.

✓ **V**—Value the plans you make and be motivated to complete the tasks you decided to work on.

✓ **E**—Envision the outcome

✓ **R**—Review the progress accordingly

Conclusion:

Goal setting is a process that starts with careful consideration of what you want to achieve. While pursuing your goals you may encounter road-blocks or obstacles. Never get discouraged; be determined to keep going all the way. Roadblocks do not mean you have failed, and failing does not mean *you* are a failure. You are capable of achieving your goals if you believe in yourself and your capabilities.

Helpful steps that can assist you to achieve your goals:

❖ Decide what you need to reach that goal

❖ Develop an action plan

❖ Know who will support you in reaching your goal

❖ Stay focused on what needs to be done

❖ Work hard to complete all assignments for due dates

❖ Make an effort to attend all the training sessions required

Your future is created by the goals you develop today which will help you to survive tomorrow.

Reflection, Notes or Journal:

_____

_____

_____

_____

_____

_____

_____

_____

_____

_____

_____

_____

_____

_____

_____

_____

Nugget 8

❧

Balancing School and Social Media

WE ARE LIVING IN the 21st Century, hence, technology has become an essential part of everyone's life, but more so in the lives of our teens. This however can interrupt the most important things in their lives. Teens are exposed to multiple platforms of communication and different electronics, of which they are excellent at operating. In several cases these social media platforms (Twitter, Snapchat, Instagram, Skype, Facebook, Tik Tok, WhatsApp, and others) seem to become the teachers in our homes. While I believe social media has its place in teenagers' lives, it should not be overused. If technology is not managed properly, it may cause you to lose focus of the most important aspect of your life, which is your education. Therefore, teens and their parents should work on a plan that can serve as a guide as to the amount of time that is spent on social media, especially during homework and family time.

Interestingly, I read with concern that some teens are getting less than 8 hours of sleep due to being on social media. This may not be healthy for teenagers, who are developing physically and emotionally at such a rapid pace. Balancing technology and getting enough sleep are two indicators that can be helpful for teenagers to do their best in school. Therefore, one key question for teenagers would be: "Are you able to manage and balance the use of technology with your schoolwork and other areas of your life?"

Suggestions that can be helpful to balance schoolwork and technology:

❖ Try to use social media with a sense of responsibility

❖ Limit the number of platforms you download if they are affecting your life in a negative way

❖ Be disciplined about when to use or when not use social media

❖ Work out a schedule for the amount of time you spend on your technology device(s)

❖ Tell yourself that your brain needs to get a certain amount of rest

❖ When it is time for bed put your phone on silent or turn it off, and keep it away from your bed—this also helps with safety

❖ Organize study time without the phone unless it is being used to enhance your study goals.

Conclusion

Social media have become an integral part of teenagers' daily activities but be careful of how it may affect your educational goals without having a structural plan for its usage. Technology has advantages and disadvantages; allow it to work for you in a positive and healthy way.

You are a star!
Keep on shining.

Reflection, Notes or Journal:

_____

_____

_____

_____

_____

_____

_____

_____

_____

_____

_____

_____

_____

_____

Nugget 9

꧁

Peer Pressure
is Real

PEER PRESSURE CAN BE viewed as participating in activities that sometimes go against your better judgment while trying to feel accepted and valued by your friends. It can also be associated with positive or negative influences. This all depends on the groups you are a part of. My years of experience working with young people have taught me that peer pressure is not just a jargon but a term which is used to describe *real* life situations that can harm pre-teens and teenagers for life. Parents are encouraged to have special talks with their teenagers about what could be negative or positive influences as they transition into teenager stage. This experience can influence your life in the right or wrong direction, but having an awareness of what peer pressure is and how to manage it can help you resist these types of pressure.

Examples of things negative peer influences may cause you to do:

- ❖ Be mean to others
- ❖ Be disrespectful to teachers
- ❖ Act like a bully
- ❖ Engage in doing drugs with friends
- ❖ Drink alcohol with friends
- ❖ Change your hairstyle
- ❖ Watch X-rated movies
- ❖ Get involved in gambling
- ❖ Engage in sexual activities
- ❖ Change the way you communicate to use scary jargon and slang
- ❖ Wear your clothes according to the fashion in style
- ❖ Adopt different walking styles

- ❖ Break rules at home and at school
- ❖ Be rude to adults without caring
- ❖ Scream/laugh while a teacher is speaking
- ❖ Belittle your friends
- ❖ Laugh at each other's dress code or hairstyles
- ❖ Skip school
- ❖ Steal from others

On the other hand, peer influence can be positive. There are some peers who will encourage each other to engage in the best practices such as:

- ✓ Studying together to get good grades on end of term exams
- ✓ No bullying
- ✓ Being involved in community services
- ✓ Being involved in sport activities
- ✓ Staying out of trouble
- ✓ Learning from each other
- ✓ Having good clean fun
- ✓ Helping each other when there is a need
- ✓ Mentoring each other to be their best self

- ✓ Being mindful of places to go or adventures to take
- ✓ Owning your values and staying true to them
- ✓ Being kind in their words and actions to teachers and peers.
- ✓ Demonstrating positive behaviors
- ✓ Holding each one responsible for their actions

Conclusion:

One way you can overcome negative peer pressure is by holding on to your values and belief systems. Never let anyone allow you to feel as if you are less than important. Be strong! The fact that peer pressure is very real and can be intense can make it difficult for you to take a stand. Nevertheless, take that stand for your life or you may fall for anything. It is never easy not to be part of a group, doing what seems to be the norm, but you can dare to be different. Your values will assist you, if you own them. My own children, while teenagers, were faced with various peer pressures, but they stood their ground and stood up with their own values. You can be an exemplary teen if you try! If things become overwhelming, reach out for help and support from your parents, and social worker at school.

What is right cannot be wrong even if your friends don't believe it's right!

Shine as bright as you can with a positive attitude. It can help you throughout your life.

Fight for what you believe in
without the fist.

Reflection, Notes or Journal:

_____

_____

_____

_____

_____

_____

_____

_____

_____

_____

Nugget 10

$$\clubsuit$$

How to be Respectful

IN SOME CULTURES, it is said that "respect and manners can take you far in life." But what is respect? It can be defined as showing regard to others and being kind in your words and actions at home, school, and in any other environment. Being respectful could also be viewed as treating others the way you want to be treated. It is therefore important for parents and other caregivers to teach children to respect others. It helps to foster good character, a great relationship, and it teaches them to consider others, as opposed to just themselves. In others words, it is like the adhesive that binds relationships.

Being respectful is to:

- ❖ Be an active listener and do so without interruptions
- ❖ Apologize when you wrong someone
- ❖ Be polite
- ❖ Be accountable for your actions
- ❖ Be thoughtful of each other's feelings
- ❖ Respect each other's boundaries
- ❖ Make decisions based on what is right
- ❖ Do not discriminate
- ❖ Practice good manners, it can help you throughout life

Conclusion:

To be respectful is to demonstrate good social skills and to treat others how you would like to be treated. It helps in providing solid foundation for all relationships.

Make an investment in your "Respect
Account" today and reap the
dividends/interest tomorrow.

Reflection, Notes or Journal:

_____

_____

_____

_____

_____

_____

_____

_____

_____

_____

_____

_____

_____

_____

Nugget 11

❧

Conflict Resolution
Tips

THE TEENAGE YEARS CAN become very intense due to experiencing various changes and moods in the body and mind, thus there may be misunderstandings which can lead to a conflict. There may be issues such as: teenagers struggling for space, independence, identity of self, being part of social groups, relationships issues, and developing close friendships. With these encounters, conflicts can occur in places such as schools with their peers and teachers, at home with siblings, or at play.

Since conflicts can take place almost anywhere and at any time, it becomes extremely important for teens to learn conflict resolution skills. Older teens seeking their independence may sometimes get into arguments with their parents over situations such as not being willing to do chores, keeping their bedrooms tidy, and going places without permission.

The following tips can be helpful for addressing conflicts:

- ❖ Always use "I" statements to express yourself
- ❖ Try staying calm when you have a disagreement with your peers or an adult
- ❖ Express yourself and be respectful
- ❖ Seek help if the conflict is intensifying
- ❖ Express yourself by sharing how you feel about the situation
- ❖ Listen to each other even if you don't feel like responding immediately
- ❖ Ask for help from a teacher, a peer counselor, or mediator to discuss the problem

❖ If you don't feel like you are in control, walk away for a moment

❖ Avoid saying harmful words you may regret later

❖ Try and be understanding of the present situation

❖ Always remember the problem is what you are working on and avoid attacking the person

❖ Do not use the blame game; instead own what you did

❖ Try not to disrespect the person with whom you have the disagreement

❖ Be free to share what is bothering you with your parents

❖ If you are unable to work through the conflict, reach out to your school counselor/social worker for support and guidance

Conclusion:

Transitioning from childhood stage to the teen-age stage can be arduous. This is sometimes due to several changes occurring at the same time within the body and mind. With hormones developing, there are times when temper tantrums may occur. When this happens, it is important that self-control and self-regulation is demonstrated during those moments.

Expressing emotions is effective when working through conflicts.

Reflection, Notes or Journal:

_____

_____

_____

_____

_____

_____

_____

_____

_____

_____

_____

_____

Nugget 12

❧

Tips for Choosing Friends

AS YOU ENTER THE teenage years, choosing friends is extremely important as you are now at the stage where interacting and socializing with peers is a key factor. Some teens may find themselves going with peers that are most popular in the school. Sometimes this can be seen in a positive and also in a negative light. It is important to note that there are good and bad friends out there and you want to be careful of those with whom you are associated. The popular crowd may not always be the best choice.

The key factor here is to choose your friends with care. Meaningful friendships should be cherished by all who are involved. Your friends should be treated with love and respect and are not to be bullied or abused in any way. Another way to choose friends wisely is to find friends with similar values, expectations, hobbies, goals, motivation, and faith-based interests.

Here are some qualities you could look for in a friend:

- ❖ Kind and caring
- ❖ Going the same places in life that you are: for example, setting goals and working toward achieving them
- ❖ Honest
- ❖ Trustworthy
- ❖ Polite and cordial
- ❖ Willing to show care and stand with you in tough moments
- ❖ Willing to tell you how they are feeling without being judgmental
- ❖ Supportive of your goals
- ❖ Sympathetic

- ❖ Warm
- ❖ Express themselves about a wrong you did and still love you
- ❖ Respectful to their teachers
- ❖ Caring and empathetic
- ❖ Comfortable in your company without any pressure
- ❖ Not bullies
- ❖ Not willing to share your story with others without permission (aka gossiping)
- ❖ Aware of your faults and still remain your friend
- ❖ One who will support you in matters of concerns

Conclusion:

True friends will not force you to get involved in wrong behaviors, or in doing anything that goes against your values. Good friends share and care in various ways whether by being your buddy, standing up for you, or just by being there for you in good and bad times. Always remember to return favors to your friends. The support of a genuine friend in time of crisis is invaluable.

Good friends are those who do not avoid you, abuse you, nor speak about you in a negative way behind your back.

Reflection, Notes or Journal:

_____

_____

_____

_____

_____

_____

_____

_____

_____

_____

_____

_____

_____

Nugget 13

Stress Management Tips

STRESS IS ONE WAY the body may respond to any kind of demand caused by good and bad encounters. Stress can be an uncomfortable experience a teenager or anyone can experience. Stress can also intensify during feelings of frustration, worry, fear, anxiety, or any other overwhelming experience. If for any reason you are experiencing any symptoms of stress, for example, intense headaches, stomachaches, lack of sleep, changes in how you socialize, difficulty concentrating, never keep it to yourself; talk to someone about how you are feeling.

Some of the most common causes of stress a teenager may experience are:

- ❖ Watching their parents arguing or fighting
- ❖ Concern about their schoolwork and grades
- ❖ Attending a new school
- ❖ Balancing assignments with extracurricular activities
- ❖ Low grades
- ❖ Facing problems with friends and peer pressure
- ❖ Worrying about the types of clothes to wear
- ❖ Not having name brand items
- ❖ Being bullied by peers
- ❖ Feeling pressured by peers to become sexually active
- ❖ Relocation to another country/community
- ❖ Changing schools and homes

❖ Going through physical and emotional changes

❖ Having problems loving and accepting themselves

❖ Watching their parents go through separation/divorce

❖ Living in unsafe neighborhoods

❖ Not being able to sleep well due to being afraid of war and crimes

❖ Dealing with financial problems as a family

❖ Being overweight or underweight

❖ Experiencing domestic violence among the adults in their homes

❖ Figuring out how to be independent

❖ Death of family members, pets, and close friends

❖ Worrying about their parents

❖ Developing relationships and love affairs

These are some tips that may help when feeling stress:

✓ Engage in physical activity whether at school or at home, like taking a walk

- ✓ Cut back on technology and rest your body and mind for a while
- ✓ Schedule some time for fun
- ✓ Be creative with your favorite hobbies and enjoy yourself
- ✓ Call a trusted friend and if you plan to visit make sure to discuss it with your parents
- ✓ Spend some time talking with your parents, laugh, and have fun. Create memories
- ✓ Learn to feel good about yourself after doing something to the best of your ability, whether in schoolwork or at home. If you feel you did a good job, be happy about it
- ✓ Take time out to listen to music
- ✓ Always express how you are feeling
- ✓ Engage in prayer and reading the Bible, it can be helpful

Conclusion:

Stress is not always a bad thing as it is the body's response to changes that create intense demands, but it can sometimes be a difficult problem to manage, especially when it becomes intensified. Whenever you find it hard to manage any form of stress-related problems, please reach out to your parents, school counselor, or social worker for support.

Reflection, Notes or Journal:

_____

_____

_____

_____

_____

_____

_____

_____

_____

_____

_____

_____

_____

_____

_____

_____

_____

_____

_____

_____

_____

Nugget 14

꧁

Dealing with Anxiety

ANXIETY CAN BE VIEWED as a feeling of worry, uneasiness, or concern about anything with an uncertain outcome. One can experience anxiety in various ways but it is characterized more by feelings of intense worry. It is normal to feel anxious about things that happen in life. Some symptoms of anxiety include sweaty palms, lightheadedness, tension, increased heart rate, and difficulty breathing.

If you find that you are having intense levels of anxiety, share your feelings with your parents who will seek help for you, or talk with your school social worker/school counselor who will further assess the situation.

Some of the below situations can cause anxiety for teenagers:

- ❖ Preparing for exams
- ❖ Taking drivers education
- ❖ Speaking before a large crowd
- ❖ Meeting new people
- ❖ Competing in sports
- ❖ Peer pressure
- ❖ Unkind friends
- ❖ Going on a date
- ❖ Keeping your GPA up
- ❖ Accidents on the road or at school
- ❖ Traumatic scenes
- ❖ Conflicts at home
- ❖ Unsafe environment/community
- ❖ Domestic violence at home
- ❖ Talking to the opposite peer for the first time
- ❖ Feeling bullied
- ❖ Violent and scary movies

Some suggestions that can assist in coping with anxiety:

- ✓ Try and be as relaxed as possible when feeling pressured
- ✓ When you are in an exam environment, take deep breaths; be calm, read it over, and begin!
- ✓ Engage in relaxation techniques, for example deep breathing exercise, meditation, and listening to calming music
- ✓ Do not aim for perfection, just do your best
- ✓ Be aware of what causes your anxiety level to increase, so you can get the help needed
- ✓ Laughter helps
- ✓ If you are home, take a nap, go for a walk, or watch something calm and relaxing
- ✓ Reach out to a professional if the anxiety level is not improving

Conclusion:

Anxiety is a normal reaction to stress related problems which can interfere with your ability to cope with everyday life. One of the best approaches is to express what you feel is causing the anxiety.

Never allow anxiety to keep you from
going after your dreams.

Reflection, Notes or Journal:

_____

_____

_____

_____

_____

_____

_____

_____

_____

_____

_____

_____

_____

_____

_____

_____

Nugget 15

✥

Tips on Managing Emotional Feelings

EMOTIONS ARE A PART of the human nature, as they serve as an indicator about what the individual might be experiencing in a given moment. During the pre-teen and teenage stage, there are physical and mental changes taking place all at once. This sometimes may cause mood swings, and can trigger some intense emotional feelings. When this happens, the best thing to do is to engage in some deep breathing exercises or share your feelings with someone. If at any time the emotions you are experiencing become over-whelming, find someone you trust and share your feelings or concerns.

Here are some simple tips that may be helpful:

❖ It is okay to name your feeling, by sharing what you are experiencing in the moment. For example, if you are feeling stressed, sad, angry, or disappointed, express those feelings by using a name tag, such as "I am feeling sad" or "I am feeling angry."

❖ Use "I" statements to express your feelings. For example, "I am feeling frustrated at this moment because of_____."

❖ Don't be afraid of your feelings—own them

❖ You can express your feeling through talking, drawing, journaling, and painting, or by taking a walk. The important thing is to release the emotions in a healthy way.

❖ Stay in touch with yourself. Do simple self-care—for example you may just need to take a long bath, get some sleep, or relax for a moment, which can be very helpful.

❖ Practice self-control, which is the ability to manage your emotions in a positive way.

❖ Talk to your school counselor if you are not coping well.

❖ Whatever you do, make every effort to be safe.

Conclusion:

Emotions are real, and can affect good relationships if not expressed in appropriate ways. One of the best approaches would be to express your feelings to avoid getting upset. If you are at school and your feelings are hurt about something or by what someone said, express what you are feeling to a peer leader, a teacher, or your school counselor/social worker. If you are home, talk with your parents. If your parents are not allowing you to express your feelings at a particular moment, try a relaxation technique which can be helpful in the calming process.

Never allow your emotions to overpower you to act irrationally. Instead, express them!

Reflection, Notes or Journal:

_____

_____

_____

_____

_____

_____

_____

_____

_____

_____

_____

_____

_____

_____

Nugget 16

❦

Self and Body-Image

SELF-IMAGE CAN BE viewed as a way in which an individual sees themselves or what they think about themselves and also what others may think of them. A key factor in helping you to maintain a positive self-image is to believe in yourself and placing value not only on how you look, but on you as a person. The skills that are helpful when you are faced with self-image concerns are: positive thinking skills, assertiveness, and self-esteem skills. In addition, try and develop a coping mechanism that will assist you in shutting out the wrong concepts about your self-image.

Body-image on a social level seems to focus more on appearances, body sizes, and shapes. This sometimes affects how a teenager may view his/herself. Television shows and magazines seem to influence what beauty is or is not. But it does not have to be accepted as the truth. The Merriam Webster dictionary defines body image as, "a subjective picture of one's own physical appearance established both by self-observation and by noting the reactions of others." The important thing to know is that you are feeling good about yourself and loving the qualities you possess. Try not to focus on the body images that are advertised on television as some of them may have been done via surgery. The holy book says "You are fearfully and wonderfully made," (Psalm 139-14). Believe what you see in your mirror, and wake up each day feeling good about who you are. Hold your head high! Accept who you are and go on with life because you are wonderful just the way you are.

Conclusion:

I am confident that all good parents have done an excellent job of telling their teens how beautiful or handsome they look. If they don't, just take a moment and look in the mirror and love yourself! Be strong, believe in yourself, your potentials, and your abilities, and simply love you and your body, no matter the shape, skin color, or size.

YOU are your own unique self.

Always remember, there is just one you.
You are unique and important. You have
purpose and you are a great gift to the
universe. You alone have your finger print;
just be your best self!

Reflection, Notes or Journal:

_____
_____
_____
_____
_____
_____
_____
_____
_____
_____

Nugget 17

❧

It is Okay to Say "I am Sorry"

IN LIFE, EVERYONE MAKES mistakes and teenagers do too. Whenever a mistake is acknowledged, it can be corrected. If you offend your friends or family members, check in to see how the situation could be handled differently to avoid repeated hurt. When this is done, apologize for what you have done wrong. It is said that females apologize easier than males. The fact is both male and female should say "I am sorry" as needed. While talking to a group of boys in a session, they shared how they felt about saying, "I am sorry." They were told that doing so shows men as being weak. But is that true? It is the opposite of course. It is a strong teenage boy or girl who, when he/she makes a mistake or hurts someone's feelings, is willing to say "I am sorry." Starting early will surely enhance your future relationship with your spouse and also prepare you to work with others. Having a better understanding about the importance of apologizing during your teenage years will further prepare you for all aspects of your adult life.

Whenever you realize you may have hurt someone, try these simple suggestions:

- ❖ Talk about the issue with the individual you hurt
- ❖ Be honest about the problem
- ❖ Admit to your mistakes without using "but"
- ❖ Take responsibility for your actions
- ❖ Express your feelings and say "I am Sorry"

Conclusion:

Always remember, mistakes happen but it is how you deal with the situations that will decide the outcome.

Whenever you apologize, you are conveying a positive message to those you hurt that you were not happy with your action. It can be rewarding!

Reflection, Notes or Journal:

_____

_____

_____

_____

_____

_____

_____

_____

_____

_____

_____

_____

_____

Nugget 18

❧

Feelings of Aloneness

LONELINESS CAN BE DEFINED as a worrying moment that occurs when an individual connection to social relationships such as family and friends are less than desired. In such a case, isolation can occur and can sometimes lead to emotional stress.

Some practical ways to manage loneliness can be:

- ❖ Express how you are feeling to a caring individual
- ❖ Stay active

❖ Read, exercise, play, and have fun
❖ Get involved in positive groups at school, in your community, or at church
❖ Be involved in community services
❖ Find peers with whom you can share humor and fun
❖ Get involved in games, sports, and clubs
❖ Be committed to your club meetings and show up
❖ Visit a family member (example, cousins, Grandma, Grandpa, uncles, and aunts) who will share history or life stories you can learn from
❖ Help with chores around the home to keep you energetic and busy
❖ Use social media with care
❖ Watch interesting television programs
❖ Visit a park with your parents' permission and walk with company
❖ Play games with and without the use of technology
❖ Get involved in youth ministry at your church

Conclusion:

Loneliness for any long period of time can lead to other mental issues. If for any reason, you feel lonely and find it difficult to cope, speak with a professional at school and your parents who will assist you to get the help you need. Do not keep it to yourself.

It's okay to like your own company and be happy with you.

Reflection, Notes or Journal:

_____

_____

_____

_____

_____

_____

_____

_____

_____

_____

Nugget 19

❧

Self-Empowerment Skills

SELF-EMPOWERMENT SKILLS OFFER techniques and tools that can assist teenagers to work effectively through life's demands and challenges. These skills can also enhance your personal growth and development in an operative way. Empowerment skills can also help you to develop a good attitude toward life and in a social context. When you have excellent self-empowerment skills, you also develop other skills, such as:

Self-orientation skills can help you in understanding who you are, your individuality, and how you react in that space.

Conflict Resolution skills can help you in making decisions as to how to solve problems using a step by step process: Take a deep breath, then:

1. Identify the main cause of the problem
2. Listen to the other person's story
3. Think of ways to resolve the situation
4. Make the best decision in the resolution process
5. Seek help if the problem becomes more challenging

Refusal skill is the ability to say No with an active voice so that individuals know you are serious about your decision.

Empathy skills are about showing care and concern toward your family members, friends, and others.

Self-direction skills help in displaying a good balance of self-control and how to take responsibility for your own actions/behaviors.

Social skills assist in communicating and interacting with your peers and others.

Expression skills can assist in expressing yourself and your emotions freely without feeling afraid.

Listening skill is paying attention when someone is speaking to you and being able to respond accordingly.

Conversation skills can assist in you in articulating what you would like to share and help you to listen attentively to others. It also helps in providing and receiving feedback.

Decision making skills can help you to think carefully about the decisions you are making about the present situation at hand and make choices. It also allows for teens to look at options and alternatives to deal with that situation.

Self-care skills help you to be self-reliant in areas such as taking care of your physical (good hygiene), and emotional health.

Daily living skills help you to do the basic things that allow you to function in life, for example, personal grooming, laundry, cooking, landscaping, and other self and home chores.

Organizational skills help you to create a planner to stay organized with daily activities which can help you to avoid procrastination.

Problem solving skill is the process of working through the details of a given *problem* to reach a solution.

Self-regulation skills help in managing your emotions in a healthy way. It is close to self-control as it also assists in managing anger and disappointments.

Conclusion:

Being knowledgeable about how to use these skills will further equip you in navigating life in a positive way. You may not always have control over the things that happen to you in life, but you can be in control of how you respond to life challenges from an early stage.

There will always be opportunities for you, but if you are not focused, they can pass you by.

Reflection, Notes or Journal:

_____

_____

_____

_____

_____

_____

_____

_____

_____

_____

_____

_____

_____

Nugget 20

⚜

The Danger of Online Acquaintances

THE INTERNET PLAYS AN important role in the life of teenagers, especially for learning, and staying in touch with parents and friends, yet it can also be a danger zone. Many predators are using this opportunity to lure young people into doing the wrong things via the internet, such as pornography, human trafficking, drugs, prostitution, and scamming. Parents should be aware of the kinds of social media their teenagers use and be proactive in equipping them with adequate information about internet use and how to ensure personal safety. Teens at all times should be careful of strangers, especially those who will promise financial gains and offer fake opportunities.

Be aware of strangers online, do not allow them to lure you into doing the wrong things. Be vigilant and say No. Report the matter to your parents or just log off.

Tips on how to avoid online predators:

❖ Do not tell strangers online where you live

❖ Don't tell them where you go to school

❖ Never go to meet anyone in secret in the name of love or blind dates

❖ Be careful how you post your personal information and photos online

❖ Do not give out any personal information about yourself or your family

❖ Do not accept gifts from strangers

❖ Stay away from certain websites such as dating sites and cultish websites because this is where predators look for their next victim

Conclusion:

While the internet is a type of socialization, it is important that you are very alert, sensitive, and smart about what you say or do. Please talk with your parents about any concerns you may have. They are the adults in your life, and they want you to be safe.

Reflection, Notes or Journal:

_____

_____

_____

_____

_____

_____

_____

_____

_____

_____

_____

_____

_____

_____

_____

_____

_____

_____

_____

_____

_____

_____

Nugget 21

꧁

Technology vs. Family Time

FAMILY TIME IS DIMINISHING as the use of technology increases. Technology is making a serious change in the way parents and children communicate and/or spend time together. During a discussion with parents of teens, some shared that they were spending less time with their teens at home because of technology. They claimed some teens even avoid chores and family time just so that they can spend more time on social media. While the media may provide entertainment or fun time, it would be a nice gesture to spend a little less time with your devices and consider spending time with your family.

Conclusion:

While parents understand the impact of the use of cell phones and other technological devices, there are other areas of life that are very important such as play time, sitting around the table for dinner time, discussions, family outings, laughing with each other, as well as talking to and learning from each other. Be mindful that family time is about creating memories and sharing great experiences.

Some of the best memories of life are made
at home with family.

Reflection, Notes or Journal:

_____

_____

_____

_____

_____

_____

_____

_____

_____

_____

_____

_____

_____

_____

_____

Nugget 22

֎

The Effects of Using Drugs

DRUG ABUSE CAN BE viewed as a habitual be-havior by an individual using illegal drugs. Teenagers sometimes assume that engaging in the use of drugs will let them feel like a grown man or woman. The fact is, being exposed to any form of drugs can have serious implications in re-gard to your growth and development mentally, physically, and academically. Drug abuse can cripple your ability to live a healthy life. These are some facts researchers reported about what drugs can do:

Drugs can:

- ❖ Impede with your ability to function well in life
- ❖ Create learning problems
- ❖ Cause physical and emotional stress
- ❖ Allow for poor judgment for those who are driving which can lead to serious accidents
- ❖ Cause problems within the family dynamics
- ❖ Create a loss of interest in normal everyday activities
- ❖ Cause mental health issues
- ❖ Create a hyper-active brain
- ❖ Cause you to develop substance abuse disorders
- ❖ Prevent you from reaching your academic goals
- ❖ Place your life on hold

Tips that can help to stay away from drugs

- ✓ Say no to using drugs
- ✓ Stay away from those who do

- ✓ Say no to your peers or adults who may introduce you to drugs
- ✓ Think about what you are doing
- ✓ Discuss the feelings you are experiencing with your parents, a friend, or someone you trust
- ✓ Think about the consequences
- ✓ Take some time to read about the effects of drugs on your physical, mental, and emotional well-being via books or internet search.
- ✓ Ask yourself, "Is taking drugs worth it or will it destroy my life?"

Conclusion:

By way of evidence, research indicates that drugs can harm you in various ways. You are now in the prime of your life with goals to achieve. It is so important that you make right choices at this stage of your life. Do not adapt bad habits that are hard to break. I am aware of many young lives that have been destroyed because of drugs. Some are getting help, while some are not. The statistics are frightening. You can be different! Use refusal skills and say NO firmly to drugs.

Making right choices in life is effective.

Reflection, Notes or Journal:

_____

_____

_____

_____

_____

_____

_____

_____

_____

_____

_____

_____

_____

_____

_____

Nugget 23

✤

The Negative Impact of Alcohol

ALCOHOL ABUSE CAN BE defined as the habit of misusing or over-using any form of alcohol for recreational purposes. It is one of those activities that can easily captivate the mind of teens. Sometimes teenagers are tempted to try alcohol for different reasons, such as the taste, the experience, peer pressure, or mere curiosity. Be aware! Alcohol can be harmful and can affect the way you function on a daily basis. Drinking at this early stage may also cause you to develop serious health problems later in life. Be careful!

Tips that can assist:

- ❖ Drinking alcohol is really for adults
- ❖ Use refusal skills and say NO to alcohol
- ❖ Try non-alcoholic juices instead
- ❖ Think about the effects of alcohol before you start drinking
- ❖ Alcohol can cause you to become a victim of sexual assault and abuse when you are under the influence
- ❖ Take some time to read about the effects of alcohol on your well-being
- ❖ It can interfere with your academic achievements and your life in general

Conclusion:

If you find you are developing the habit of drinking, talk with your school counselor or social worker who can develop intervention plans to help you before it gets to the addiction stage.

See life challenges as an opportunity to
make you stronger.

Reflection, Notes or Journal:

_____

_____

_____

_____

_____

_____

_____

_____

_____

_____

_____

_____

_____

_____

_____

Nugget 24

⚜

Developing Good
Saving Habits

MANY PARENTS TRY TO instill the habit of saving in their child from an early age. My parents gave me a saving jar, and I gave my children piggy-banks in their younger days so that they developed the habit of saving. With today's technology, some teenagers can get debit cards and start working part-time and on holidays by the age of 16 in some cultures. This gives them the opportunity to keep depositing in their accounts and save toward important things that they love, while some will save certain amount for a particular item.

Tips that can help in saving:

- ❖ Be creative and save even small amounts
- ❖ Save from your allowances and pocket money received from uncle, aunts, grandparents, and parents
- ❖ Save from your part-time jobs (depending your age and culture)
- ❖ Create your own individual spending budget before you go shopping, especially with friends
- ❖ Be aware of friends who will pressure you into purchasing only name brand items
- ❖ Do not put pressure on yourself—just save whenever you can

Conclusion:

Saving from an early age is extremely important. It allows for some independence where you are able to purchase items of your choice. Developing the art of saving also teaches you how to save as an adult later on in life.

Saving a dollar today, can amount to millions
in the future! You will be glad you did!

Reflection, Notes or Journal:

_____

_____

_____

_____

_____

_____

_____

_____

_____

_____

_____

_____

_____

_____

_____

_____

Nugget 25

❧

Don't be a Bully or a Victim

BULLYING CAN BE DEFINED as being intentionally mean toward others. This type of behavior has become a real issue in the lives of many teenagers at schools and in the community at large. Some of the reasons that may create this type of behavior could be due to the environmental factors teens may be exposed to. Be aware of friends at school who may behave as if they are the boss on the block. You might see these bullies as bosses because they behave as being famous. However, in reality they may be very weak and may be experiencing low self-esteem issues and are afraid. Bullying is wrong and should not be condoned.

Tips on how not to be a bully:

❖ Be open to meet new friends
❖ Treat each other with respect
❖ Show care toward each other
❖ Treat everyone equally
❖ Be empathetic
❖ Be kind to each other
❖ Use your words to express your feelings
❖ Learn and have fun at school
❖ Be mindful of other people's differences
❖ If you are constantly mean toward your friends, seek help. Talk with your social worker, teacher, or school counselors.

How not to be a victim:

✓ Use your voice and say No to bullies
✓ Do not be afraid—stand up and report them to your teachers
✓ Do not accept any form of bullying

✓ Let your parents know what you are experiencing and encourage them to report it to your school immediately

Conclusion:

Bullying is wrong and should not be tolerated. On your first day of school, do **not** be afraid, try and develop the strength to have a zero tolerance toward bullying. Always remember, some students may act as a bully because they were bullied too. "Hurt teens sometimes hurt others." Say No to bullying!

Bullying is not a strength; it is more a
weakness!

Reflection, Notes or Journal:

_____

_____

_____

_____

_____

_____

_____

_____

_____

_____

_____

_____

_____

_____

_____

_____

Nugget 26

❧

Teens'
Expectations of
Parents

PARENTS HAVE HIGH EXPECTATIONS for their children and likewise children have expectations of their parents. But for this to be applicable, teenagers will have to try and adhere the best way they can. Teenagers should be allowed the opportunity to share how they feel about an expectation.

The following expectations can be read as the voice of a teenager. I would like my parents to:

- ❖ Love me, no matter what
- ❖ Communicate with me in good and bad times
- ❖ Be respectful of my space
- ❖ Never compare me with my siblings or with other individuals; each child is different and has his/her own unique qualities
- ❖ Set reasonable expectations of me
- ❖ Listen to me with an open mind
- ❖ Avoid negative criticism, instead be constructive and offer suggestions
- ❖ Recognize that I have real feelings
- ❖ Not to embarrass me in front of my friends or teachers
- ❖ Set rules and boundaries in a respectful way
- ❖ Not label, threaten, or abuse me in any way

- ❖ Attend Parent-teachers' meetings and extracurricular activities whenever you can. I am always looking out for you!
- ❖ Be a role model to me in all you do
- ❖ Set clear guidelines for both girls and boys without being partial
- ❖ Be authentic in your relationship and in your faith
- ❖ Support me both emotionally and financially the best way you can
- ❖ Express your concerns without any harm
- ❖ Respect my privacy, unless there is a real need to invade it
- ❖ Be aware of my sensitive moments
- ❖ Recognize that yelling hurts and I prefer calm instructions and conversations
- ❖ Be careful of your jokes or teasing
- ❖ Offer praise for trying, for example, completed tasks, good behaviors, and achievements, even if it is not up to your standards at the moment
- ❖ Be there for me even when I behave as if I don't care

- ❖ Don't yell at me when my grades are not good, but encourage me to do better
- ❖ Motivate me to be my best, and work with me at my level of achievement
- ❖ Check in with me and find out what might be going on at school which could be the reasons for my low or high achievements
- ❖ Recognize that I can be a little self-conscious and easily embarrassed; please be supportive as I go through these changes as I grow up
- ❖ Always remember to keep me in your thoughts, and in your prayers
- ❖ Be my parents and not my best buddy, it can give mixed signals sometimes
- ❖ Acknowledge my limitations and help me overcome them
- ❖ Don't abuse me physically, mentally, sexually, or emotionally. It is wrong! It hurts!
- ❖ When talking about sex and prevention of sex, don't give me parables; let the

information flow by talking casually and real. Remember I am growing up.

Conclusion:

The teenage years can be challenging and often it can be difficult to maintain a reasonable or good relationship with parents during this time even though not all teenagers will be affected in this area. Nevertheless, it is important that parents try and work together with their teens in order to build and have the best relationships ever. This will also allow for the greatest memories to develop with each other. In moments when undesired behaviors are displayed, parents should always try to show empathy, patience, guidance and love for their teenagers. They will always remember it.

Family relationship is everything.
Maintain and cherish the one you have with
your parents.

Reflection, Notes or Journal:

_____

_____

_____

_____

_____

_____

_____

_____

_____

_____

_____

_____

_____

_____

_____

Nugget 27

❧

Things I Want My Parents to Know

THE TEENAGE STAGE CAN be a rough patch as your child is going through rapid physical and emotional changes. But this is the time they need the support of their parents even though they may behave as if they don't need it.

Teenagers are sometimes unwilling to share their innermost feelings with their parents, maybe because of the level of their relationship. It is however a key factor for parents and teens to build and maintain a good relationship so you will be able to share things that may be affecting you.

For teens who may not be able to say what is on their minds to their parents, here are some things teens would like their parents to know:

- ❖ It is sometimes hard to be a teenager
- ❖ School work is sometimes difficult and challenging
- ❖ Talking to a boy does not means he is my boyfriend and we are in a relationship
- ❖ Talking to a girl does not means she is my girlfriend and we are in a relationship
- ❖ Sometimes it feels challenging when my friends are sharing where they go and what they do and I choose not to go because I am trying to be obedient
- ❖ When I am bullied and I may still have to go to school every day, it is hard
- ❖ Some subjects are difficult to manage and I still have to sit in that class where I often feel so lost

- ❖ When I am pressured to get involved in sexual activities and I say NO, my friends sometimes laugh
- ❖ Not all my friends are bad influences on me
- ❖ I will make mistakes sometimes
- ❖ I am not on social media at all times to do the wrong things; I go on to stay informed, to play games, and to have my space
- ❖ I am not interested in playing the sports or the extracurricular activities you prefer
- ❖ You never ask me if this is what I want to do, instead you tell me what I must become; please encourage me instead
- ❖ It is best if you talk with me because time-out sometimes does not work
- ❖ I know the generation gap is a challenge, but bear with me
- ❖ You may think I don't know about love and relationships, but I do. Guide me instead of being mad.

- ❖ Sometimes parents are wrong, but that's okay. I know you mean well. It would be nice for you to say though, that you are sorry, or just acknowledge it. We all make mistakes, right?
- ❖ If you can, do not yell. Instead, talk or ask questions. I will answer
- ❖ I love you dearly, words cannot express even if I don't always show it
- ❖ Remember, sometimes I do get moody. Be patient with me.

Conclusion:

Thank you for believing in me. Sometimes teenagers may seem reserved but they still need their parents.

Remember to tell your parents how much
you love them!

Reflection, Notes or Journal:

_____

_____

_____

_____

_____

_____

_____

_____

_____

_____

_____

_____

_____

_____

_____

_____

Nugget 28

❧

Should I Listen to My Parents?

SOMETIMES TEENS ARE OF the view that they should do whatever they choose to do without any guidance. But is this always a wise thing to do? Good parents, in most cases, want the best for their children. At times, the care and love parents show may be misinterpreted by their teenager as some sort of bondage or a mere act of being over-protective. There is the need, though, for teens to listen to their parents, so they can be guided throughout this important journey of their life.

Here are some reasons why you should listen to your parents:

- ❖ They love you
- ❖ They genuinely do care about you
- ❖ They have your best interest at heart
- ❖ They've got your back
- ❖ You are living in their home
- ❖ They want the best for you
- ❖ They are supporting you
- ❖ They have lots of experiences
- ❖ They are older than you
- ❖ They are the ones sending you to school
- ❖ If you get into trouble, the first person you or the police call will be your parents

Conclusion:

When your parents feel connected to your daily life, they will be able to understand you better and help you through challenging moments. Good parents are motivated to help their children become successful citizens. For some teens, a parent and child relationship may not exist, and you may find these tips unnecessary, but don't be discouraged. If there is someone who demonstrates a parental type relationship or one who is influential in your life, try to communicate and listen to that person. It can be helpful. I have had the privilege of working with and mentoring students throughout their teenage years, and I have found that many teens are sometimes afraid or hesitant to share their problems with their parents due to fear of consequences. Nevertheless, it is extremely imperative that you and your parents work on building a bond so that no matter what happens, or what trouble you are in, or whatever you may be struggling with, you will be able to talk with your parents.

"Be positive about life, and stay away from all negative influences that may come your way."

"Be optimistic about your life even if no one else is."

Reflection, Notes or Journal:

_____

_____

_____

_____

_____

_____

_____

_____

_____

_____

_____

_____

Nugget 29

꧁

Parents' Concerns

TEENAGERS ARE SOMETIMES concerned about the things their parents may have a problem dealing with. The way to creatively handle these issues is to be aware of them. It is essential to get to know your parents' likes and dislikes and most importantly, be reminded of the home rules. Most parents desire a positive and healthy relationship with their teenagers amidst some of the struggles.

These are some items that may be of concern to your parents:

- ❖ When you disobey rules at home and at school
- ❖ When you are disrespectful and do not listen
- ❖ When you show little interest in your schoolwork
- ❖ When you bring your friends over without permission
- ❖ When your friends destroy their property
- ❖ When you play loud music and disturbs others
- ❖ When you spend more time on your cell phone than on your homework
- ❖ When your clothes are on the floor all over the room
- ❖ When you make plans to stay out late and go to parties without permission
- ❖ When you focus more on having an intimate relationship than on getting good grades

- ❖ When you demonstrate mean-spirited behaviors
- ❖ When you talk at your parents in a disrespectful way
- ❖ When you leave home to go on road trips without discussing it with your parents.

Conclusion:

Parents think differently in regard to life issues, situations, and surroundings. This is understandable with age and maturity, but as teenagers, one way to develop a great relationship with your parents is to be respectful, open, honest, and take responsibility for your actions. Take it easy on your parents so you both can enjoy each other for a long time.

Never underestimate the power of the
words that are spoken.

Reflection, Notes or Journal:

_____

_____

_____

_____

_____

_____

_____

_____

_____

_____

_____

_____

_____

_____

_____

_____

Nugget 30

❧

Freedom—From a Teenager Point of View

ALL TEENAGERS WISH FOR their freedom, but are they really ready? Freedom for teenagers may look different for each individual due to culture, environment, and belief systems. In a discussion with some teenagers on the topic of what freedom means to them, these were some their responses:

❖ "I am looking forward to my independence as soon as I reach a certain age"

- ❖ A time to explore
- ❖ Going to college
- ❖ "Doing my own thing in my own time"
- ❖ "My parents are too over-protective"

I can see why teenagers want to be independent as it can be a good feeling and a part of growing into emergent adults. Teenagers may want the freedom to have some sense of control over what they do, where they go, and who they choose to be their friends. But it does take time, with a level of preparedness, responsibility and maturity. There is a time and season for all aspects of life.

Conclusion:

Real freedom is an opportunity where teenagers can learn more about themselves and interact well with others. Take into consideration that freedom and independence come with a certain amount of responsibility, time, and age.

Reflection, Notes or Journal:

_____

_____

_____

_____

_____

_____

_____

_____

_____

_____

_____

_____

_____

_____

_____

_____

_____

_____

_____

_____

Nugget 31

※

Am I Really Ready to be a Parent?

THE ROLE OF A parent comes with responsibilities that are not recommended for teenagers. You are unique and you don't need to behave like everyone else. In fact, some of your peers are setting themselves up for failure, and some are even afraid to be their true self. Before long, some teens may want to engage in unprotected sex in order to be able to tell their stories too. Take a moment and think about the consequences that follow when you are involved in such activity. This is where you can stand out and stand up for what you would like to achieve in life. You will be glad you waited!

Use refusal skills and say **NO** to risky behaviors. Take into consideration the various diseases and the risk of getting pregnant or becoming a parent too early. Babies can wait for the right time and with the right person. The teenage stage should be used for goal setting, career awareness, extracurricular activities, having fun, and enjoying the blessings of their Creator without becoming a teen parent. Empower yourself with knowledge through reading on the matter of abstinence and making good choices.

Conclusion:

As teens, you are encouraged to be realistic about the decisions you make on a daily basis. Stay in school and get an education. With such achievements, teenagers can live the life they love as they grow older. Becoming a father or a mother as a teenager has ramifications and setbacks.

One question you can use as you do some reflections is to ask yourself, **"What do I want to** achieve now for myself so that I can plan better for the future?"

———

There is more to life than becoming a teenage parent. Remember parenting comes with lots of responsibilities!

———

Reflection, Notes or Journal:

_____

_____

_____

_____

_____

_____

_____

_____

_____

_____

_____

_____

_____

_____

Motivational Quotes

You are an important part of the architecture of your life. Whatever you do with your life can affect your building. Building here could be viewed as your life and can be affected in a negative or positive way.

Never quit. If you fall, get up, and go!

Always bear in mind that obstacles provide steps to go higher.

Life is filled with challenges, but what really matters is how you react to them.

Whenever you experience difficult moments or if you failed at something, do not be discouraged but keep on trying.

Do all you can to be the best you can without pressuring yourself too much.

It's okay not to be perfect. Instead, rise to your highest potential.

Stand up and be yourself instead of trying so hard to squeeze into a frame that is just not your fit.

Life is like a camera; focus on what you see, describe it, love it, and take care of it for that picture is you.

It is more precious to be yourself than to lose yourself.

Make your teenage years count.

The stars in the sky are there to light up the sky, you can light up your world.

Self-Esteem
Quiz

Mark true or false to each of the following statements:

I accept myself and I feel good about me ___

Others are better than I am ___

I enjoy socializing with others ___

I deserve love and respect ___

I feel valued ___

Being myself is important ___

I make friends easily ___

I find it difficult to make friends ___

I am strong enough to deal with criticisms ___

I am not strong and I can't cope with negative critics ___

I speak up for myself, and share my views ___

I am a happy person ___

I am a carefree person ___

I don't worry about what others say about me ___

I feel respected ___

I don't feel respected ___

I am a confident person ___

I enjoy helping others ___

I don't need other's approval to feel good about myself ___

I am happy for other's success ___

Identify the statements that make you feel good about yourself and validate them. For those you may have a little concern about, don't worry too much, they can be worked on.

If you are experiencing any challenges in an over-whelming way, reach out to someone for help. Talk with your parents, your school counselor, your social worker, or a community pastor.

Words in Action

Active: engage in daily activities

Ambitious: the desire to be successful in life

Assertive: being able to state your needs and opinions clearly in a respectful way without becoming angry

Cheerfulness: having a state of mind which is positive and happy

Confidence: believing in yourself in a way that decreases shyness

Cautious: being careful and aware of dangers lurking around

Enthusiasm: the emotion you will feel when you are extremely happy about doing something

Extroverted: enjoy socializing with people around you

Gratitude: is about appreciating the people and the things in your life

Hopeful: you are feeling and believing in things that can change or be better

Interest: feeling concern or curious about something, a person, or a place

Kindness: being considerate, generous, and friendly to others

Optimistic: feeling or showing hope for the future

Persistence: the ability to stay focused in times of discouragement

Reserved: not willing to share your thoughts with others immediately

Resilient: able to withstand difficult moments in life

Serious: no-nonsense kind of behavior

Trustworthy: dependable and honest

Vibrant: energetic and excited with enthusiasm

Personal Qualities for Life

Caring: A desire to help
Determination: Having the will-power to act or do something
Considerate: Thinking of others
Motivation: Enthusiastic
Compassion: The ability to recognize the difficulties others are going through
Curious: Eager to learn more
Polite: Exhibiting good manners
Kind: Thoughtful, caring
Pleasant: Being polite
Sincere: Being honest

Hardworking: Putting a lot of effort into a job well done

Self-reliant: Able to do or decide things for yourself

Bible Verses for Encouragement

Jeremiah 29-11

For I know the thoughts that I think toward you, saith the LORD, thoughts of peace, and not of evil, to give you an expected end.

Psalms 134- 14

I will praise thee; for I am fearfully and wonderfully made: marvellous are thy works; and that my soul knoweth right well.

Philippians 4-13

I can do all things through Christ which strengtheneth me.

1Corinthians9-24

Know ye not that they which run in a race run all, but one receiveth the prize? So run, that ye may obtain.

Ecclesiastes 12-1

Remember now thy Creator in the days of thy youth, while the evil days come not, nor the years draw nigh, when thou shalt say, I have no pleasure in them.

Proverbs 20-11

Even a child is known by his doings, whether his work is pure, and whether it be right.

References

Kenneth R. Ginsburg & Jablow M.M. (2011)
Building Resilience in children and teens

Brain Development, Teen Behavior and Preventing Drug Use, Feb 2021, retrieved from:
http://www.drugfree.org/why-do-teens-act-this-way/

Mental-health-matters.com (2017)

This book is prepared solely for informational and educational purposes, and not for therapy. Please seek professional help for any issues you are facing that are overwhelming.

Reflection, Notes or Journal:

_____

_____

_____

_____

_____

_____

_____

_____

_____

_____

_____

_____

_____

_____

_____

_____

_____

_____

_____

Acknowledgement

I honor the Lord for His guidance and his help every step of the way while working on this project. My heartfelt thanks to my editing pals Patrice and Latona for their kind help and expertise. To my family I say thanks for your patience and encouragements. To my colleagues who offered their suggestions, thank you all for your kind encouragements, support, and technical help.

About the Author

Murween Perry-Rose lives with her family in Illinois. She considers her faith and her family to be most important to her. When she is not spending time with the Lord, and her family, she's writing something to help various groups of individuals, and young people are one of her passions. Murween has years of experience as a school counselor working with children and teenagers. She is also a mental health counselor.

www.ingramcontent.com/pod-product-compliance
Lightning Source LLC
Chambersburg PA
CBHW061723020426
42331CB00006B/1067